THIRTY DEVOS THAT

BUILD

A BOLDER MAN

VINCE MILLER

THIRTY DEVOS THAT
BUILD A BOLDER MAN

Published by Resolute
Interior Design and Layout: Gretchen Miller
Cover Design and Layout: Eric Beavers

First Edition: 2018

ISBN: 978-0-9993525-4-0

Library of Congress Control Number: 2018961544

Printed in the United States of America

TO: _____

FROM: _____

NOTE: _____

_____

_____

_____

_____

_____

A NOTE FROM THE AUTHOR

I pray this devotional will benefit your life and your spiritual growth as a man. I hope you will do three things as you engage each time. First, I pray that you will be receptive to the Word of God. I love it when men dig into the Bible. The Bible is not an ordinary book; it is the means of discovering God and spiritual transformation, but it requires a receptive man. Second, lean into brotherhood by inviting another man to join with you. Build a friendship, share transparently, and have conversations that go beyond the superficial and shallow conversations we have every day. Consider sharing the devotionals that impact you with others. Third, put into action what you have learned. Choose an action item each time, knowing that one small step each day leads to long success over a lifetime.

Keep moving forward,

Vince Miller

ABOUT RESOLUTE

WE DISCIPLE & DEVELOP MEN TO LEAD

We believe men are a strategic audience and force for change in the world and that God ordained men with power, authority, and the opportunity to define the world around them. While the culture would attempt to silence the voice of men by attacking their masculinity, exaggerating male shortcomings, and belittling their Christian worldview, we believe this is not the answer. The answer is to build better men. When we build better men, we build better homes, marriages, workplaces, and churches. When one man gets better, everyone gets better.

But we have an enemy.

The enemy is not the culture, opposing beliefs, media, politics, or even pornography. The enemy is apathy. The appeal of inaction lies within every man's heart, enticing him to say nothing and do nothing when God has called him to action. At Resolute, after leading thousands of men through mentoring, we have found no greater obstacle to spiritual formation. We believe that God wants to develop a new brotherhood of men, but first he needs to find men willing to defy their passive inclinations.

At Resolute, we provide men with easy-to-use tools that help them fight the impulse of apathy. Here are a few.

1. **ON YOUR OWN | THE MEN'S DAILY DEVOTIONAL** is our tool for getting men into the Bible daily. This is the tool you hold in your hand. Read more about it here: www.beresolute/mdd.

2. **ONE ON ONE | THIRTY VIRTUES THAT BUILD A MAN** is our tool for helping men grow in their faith and biblical understanding through accountability relationships. You should optimally read through this material alongside another Christian man. As you find new opportunities to mentor or be mentored by others, you can return to this tool and use it again. You can find it at www.beresolute.org/thirty.

3. **IN A GROUP | MEN'S GROUP CONTENT** is for leading a group of men. There is no faster way to grow in your faith than to step out in leadership. We offer small group videos for leaders and handbooks for participants. See our full library of videos here: www.beresolute.org/videos.

AUTHOR & SPEAKER VINCE MILLER

Abandoned by his drug-using father at the age of two, Vince Miller grew up in a challenging and anxiety-producing environment. He endured the strain of his mother's two failed marriages as well as her poor choices and drug use. Fortunately, during Vince's formative teen years his grandfather, a man of faith, stepped up to mentor Vince, guiding him through a particularly difficult period.

Though he resisted initially, Vince surrendered his life to Christ at the age of 20. Soon after, he stood by his grandfather on his deathbed as cancer took his life. At that time, Vince committed before God to give back by mentoring men as his grandfather had mentored him. As Vince's story demonstrates, mentors play a vital role in helping men overcome the enormous hurdles presented by manhood, mentoring, fathering, and leadership —equipping them to live right before God.

Audiences respond to Vince's stories and teaching that motivate, convict, and sometimes even shock. He inspires men to lead, mentor, and disciple others with an intelligent argument for faith, inspiring presentation of the gospel, and stories of choices he made as a man, husband, and father. His compelling story of the problem and need for building better men has impassioned thousands of men to live with greater conviction and become the men God intended them to be. Prepare to be challenged with his message entitled, "Build Better Men."

After serving in notable ministry organizations for over 25 years (including Young Life, InterVarsity, TCU Football, and Eagle Brook Church), Vince founded Resolute, a non-profit organization focused on providing men with tools for discipleship and mentorship.

He currently lives in St. Paul, Minnesota, with Christina, his wife. They have three children—Faith, Grant, and Riley. Vince is an authentic and transparent leader who loves to communicate to men and has a deep passion for God's Word. He has authored numerous books and small-group guides for men, and he is the primary creator of all Resolute content and training materials. See Vince's profile here: www.beresolute.org/vince-miller.

USING THIRTY DEVOS

THE PURPOSE

This 30-lesson devotional is for men to use in private reflection or conversations with other men. It is written to invite character development conversations for men of any age, as well as spiritual development, and can be used repeatedly.

THE PROCESS

1 | BUILD YOURSELF

Read through one virtue each week and answer the questions within the lesson. Each lesson uses our B.U.I.L.D. process.

- **BEGIN** with the goal in the text.
- **UNPACK** your thoughts and issues.
- **INFORM** from the Bible.
- **LAND** on action steps.
- **DO** one action for one week.

2 | BROTHER UP

Take each lesson further by partnering up with another man. Use the 30 lessons as a mentoring and discipleship tool that takes all the guesswork out of a spiritual conversation. Brother up with a friend, neighbor, church member, associate, or relative.

THE PAYOFF

If you stay with the process for all 30 lessons, you will grow in character as a man of God. Often, men just need a plan to get moving spiritually. This book is a plan—a method and a process that results in outcomes with a rich spiritual payoff.

TABLE OF CONTENTS

INVITED

While walking by the Sea of Galilee, he saw two brothers, Simon (who is called Peter) and Andrew his brother, casting a net into the sea, for they were fishermen, and he said to them, "Follow me, and I will make you fishers of men." Immediately they left their nets and followed him. Matthew 4:18-20

An invitation into the inner circle has a powerful attraction for men. Call to mind any situation where you received an "exclusive" invite. When a compelling opportunity presents itself, and you are invited to join in the undertaking, it is difficult to resist.

Every man is just one invitation away from a great adventure. And it is Jesus who invites all men into the greatest experience of their lives. He asks a man to give up his current situation in exchange for a life of discipleship. For some men the call to follow is subtle, and for others the call is much more apparent and challenging. In the case of Peter and Andrew, it meant walking away from their established lifestyle and occupation and embracing a radically different experience. Even without fully understanding the call, they obeyed and began the great adventure of their lives.

God, often I don't take the time to reflect on the little invitations you extend to me. Today I commit to listening to your call and following where you lead regardless of the cost.

B
_____

BEGIN: Why is this text so important?

U
_____

UNPACK: What issues do you need to address?

I
_____

INFORM: What does the text say to do?

L
_____

LAND: What steps do you need to take?

D
_____

DO: What action will you take today?

BREAKDOWN

Search me, God, and know my heart; test me and know my anxious thoughts.
See if there is any offensive way in me, and lead me in the way everlasting.
Psalm 139:23-24

Entropy is defined as a progressive decline into disorder. It's a process of breakdown over time that eventually leads to weakening, dysfunction, and collapse. For example, consider the oil additive in your engine. If you go beyond the recommended usage limits of the oil in your vehicle, then entropy occurs. The oil becomes saturated with engine gunk which breaks down its ability to adequately lubricate the engine. This results in friction and eventually seizure if not addressed. The same law is at work in all areas of life, including the spiritual life.

Over the years a man will have seasons of challenge in his spiritual life. Surely you are no stranger to the anxieties that come from these seasons. And often anxiety creates entropy that over time will gunk up your life and lead to a spiritual breakdown. The Psalmist above is reflecting on something similar. His cry to God suggests a need to rid his heart of the gunk of life that has built up over time. What you need during seasons of challenge is for God to lead you through and cleanse the heart of its anxiety and debris.

God, I often try to hide from you. This is because I do not understand my own heart. Today, God, expose my desires and the sin hidden even to me and remind me of the life you intend for me.

B

BEGIN: Why is this text so important?

U

UNPACK: What issues do you need to address?

I

INFORM: What does the text say to do?

L

LAND: What steps do you need to take?

D

DO: What action will you take today?

FIXED

Therefore, since we are surrounded by such a great cloud of witnesses, let us throw off everything that hinders and the sin that so easily entangles. And let us run with perseverance the race marked out for us, fixing our eyes on Jesus, the pioneer, and perfecter of faith. For the joy that was set before him he endured the cross, scorning its shame, and sat down at the right hand of the throne of God. Consider him who endured such opposition from sinners, so that you will not grow weary and lose heart. Hebrews 12:1-3

The North Star, known as Polaris, is a natural compass man has utilized since the dawn of seafaring. Find Polaris, lower your gaze, and you've found true north. As sailors know, navigating a sea that looks the same for hundreds of miles in all directions requires a navigational anchor.

All men are travelers. Over a lifetime you will traverse a vast landscape. You often face challenges that leave you perplexed, but there is hope because the challenges you face have been met by others, even a "great cloud of witnesses." These men that have gone before you teach you how to fix your eyes on the prize of our faith in the midst of successes and failures. Your nautical north—Jesus Christ—gives all men the right direction and proper orientation.

God, my eyes may be tempted to fix on my situations today, but I commit instead to turn them to you in the hope that you will be my guide and the perfecter of my faith. Give me direction today when I feel lost, and give me the strength to persevere when I feel weary.

B
_____

BEGIN: Why is this text so important?

U
_____

UNPACK: What issues do you need to address?

I
_____

INFORM: What does the text say to do?

L
_____

LAND: What steps do you need to take?

D
_____

DO: What action will you take today?

GREATER

As you come to him, a living stone rejected by men but in the sight of God chosen and precious, you yourselves like living stones are being built up as a spiritual house, to be a holy priesthood, to offer spiritual sacrifices acceptable to God through Jesus Christ. 1 Peter 2:4-5

In the Old Testament, stones had vital usage and carried rich symbolism. Stones served as tablets upon which God wrote Ten Commandments he intended generations to heed. In other instances, stones were used in battle as lethal weapons. Rocks marked boundaries, sealed tombs, and served as altars of worship for God and heathen idols. Foundations and walls were made of stone, and functioned as symbols in incredible stories that Christ told in the New Testament record. And here in the letter of First Peter, you can find yourself in this word picture. You are a living stone. You are chosen, precious, and part of a structure built by God's hand.

This image is deeply symbolic. You are part of an ancient and enduring creation, one that God continues to craft out of the members of his church. There is a purpose to this structure, and each "rock" plays a role wherever God sets it. Once merely a stone, in God's hands and in concert with the members beside you, you become something even grander, a testimony to God's glory and his divine purposes.

God, my purposes sometimes—maybe even often—take precedence over yours. But not today. Have your way with me and let's build something incredible.

BEGIN: Why is this text so important?

UNPACK: What issues do you need to address?

INFORM: What does the text say to do?

LAND: What steps do you need to take?

DO: What action will you take today?

RECIPROCATE

"As the Father has loved me, so have I loved you. Now remain in my love."
John 15:9

Jesus reveals to the world the love of God. God's love for his creation is unrelenting and unstoppable. And God demonstrates his love for us through Jesus by sending him into the world when humanity was at its worst. While we did not love Jesus, he continued to love us. He never ceased to pursue us with his love even through persecution, humiliation, beating, rejection, and crucifixion.

It may not be socially acceptable to tell another man you "love" him, but Jesus did not shy away from using this word with his men at the moments leading up to his betrayal, arrest, and execution. In this text, Jesus is sharing a final charge that accentuates the profound reciprocal love the Godhead has for his followers. We know God's love because of Jesus' love. Don't you want to know and experience real unconditional love? To be loved by another when you do not deserve it? Jesus' example is your cue to love all mankind the same. You are called to love when you are not loved—to love even those the world insists are unlovable.

God, I often withhold the love you have so freely extended to me. I confess I have only loved those who love me, and not those who don't. May I reflect your love today by loving someone that does not love me.

BEGIN: Why is this text so important?

UNPACK: What issues do you need to address?

INFORM: What does the text say to do?

LAND: What steps do you need to take?

DO: What action will you take today?

WILLING

The word of the Lord came to Jonah son of Amittai: "Go to the great city of Nineveh and preach against it, because its wickedness has come up before me." But Jonah ran away from the Lord and headed for Tarshish. He went down to Joppa, where he found a ship bound for that port. After paying the fare, he went aboard and sailed for Tarshish to flee from the Lord. Jonah 1:1-3

Often men long to hear from God. In fact, on some days we want to know precisely what he wants us to do and the direction in which he desires us to go. Explicit instruction, guidance, and purpose would seem to be helpful. It would be nice to wake up each day and have God tell you precisely what the day holds and your particular role in it; there would be comfort in knowing God's will and aligning with him. Unless, of course, you don't like what he is saying!

Jonah was one of the men God chose to involve in his mission—one of God's mouthpieces—and he served faithfully right up until he got an assignment he didn't like. Don't let yourself be offended or disheartened when God gives you a difficult task or asks you to love and serve a difficult person. Your life of discipleship will not always be easy, fun, or exactly what you want it to be. But the truth is you will always be blessed when walking in the direction that God has instructed. As you spend time reading God's Word, listening to the convictions of the Spirit, and taking steps of faith, you will discern God's leading and discover the great adventure God has for you today. If you find God is leading you somewhere you don't want to go, ask him for the courage to obey.

God, I am not always willing to do what you say. Sometimes I, like Jonah, reject your call. Hear the confessions of my heart and accept this repentance as a new sacrifice. I pray that in carrying out your will today I will receive unseen blessings.

B

BEGIN: Why is this text so important?

U

UNPACK: What issues do you need to address?

I

INFORM: What does the text say to do?

L

LAND: What steps do you need to take?

D

DO: What action will you take today?

PRAY BOLDLY

Elisha said, "Go around and ask all your neighbors for empty jars. Don't ask for just a few. Then go inside and shut the door behind you and your sons. Pour oil into all the jars, and as each is filled, put it to one side." She left him and shut the door behind her and her sons. They brought the jars to her, and she kept pouring. When all the jars were full, she said to her son, "Bring me another one." But he replied, "There is not a jar left." Then the oil stopped flowing. 2 Kings 4:3-6

Elisha was a bold man of God. He had great faith in God and did not hesitate to ask for what appeared to be humanly impossible. In the text above, a widow comes to him with a request. The widow and her sons were buried in enormous debt and faced life-altering circumstances. So Elisha instructed her to ask for empty jars, but not just a few—as many as she could find. What she didn't know was that the amount of oil God would miraculously provide directly correlated to the number of jars she was willing and able to collect.

Jesus spoke these words to his men in Matthew 7: "If you, then, though you are evil, know how to give good gifts to your children, how much more will your Father in heaven give good gifts to those who ask him!" The reality is that God wants you to ask boldly for the salvation you need and act accordingly in anticipation of his provision. Instead of asking God how he will provide, ask how you can act faithfully in light of his promises.

God, you know the desires of my heart. Without you I am nothing. Today hear the deepest desires of my heart, and answer the prayers that pour out from my soul. May I live with the certainty that you will provide, and let me act accordingly with great anticipation.

B

BEGIN: Why is this text so important?

U

UNPACK: What issues do you need to address?

I

INFORM: What does the text say to do?

L

LAND: What steps do you need to take?

D

DO: What action will you take today?

HUMBLE ACTION

Who is wise and understanding among you? Let them show it by their good life, by deeds done in the humility that comes from wisdom. James 3:13

A man is not defined or proven by what he thinks or what he says. A man is proven by what he does—by his actions. It is easy to tell others what you stand for—but your actions will reveal the truth. As the brother of Jesus, James had a front-row seat to the knowledge, teachings, and action of the Son of God. Jesus' actions proved to James the validity of the things Jesus said about himself. In the same way, your actions make it clear to others who you really are and what you really believe.

Want to prove yourself wise? James says the fruit of wisdom isn't shrewd dealings, but humble service. See the difference in character each of those actions would show? Remember that humility does not mean to adopt a low opinion of yourself, but to work to raise the standing of those around you. Reflect on the words of Paul in Philippians 2:3 today: "Rather, in humility value others above yourselves." Wisdom by nature seeks to serve and gain insight from others; self-inspired, self-serving actions betray a foolish heart.

God, I must confess my actions sometimes are only centered on what I want and desire. I pray you will give me humility as I act today, and that my actions will reflect your values and virtues so that others might know you.

B BEGIN: Why is this text so important?

U UNPACK: What issues do you need to address?

I INFORM: What does the text say to do?

L LAND: What steps do you need to take?

D DO: What action will you take today?

IMPOSSIBLE

Then the Lord said to Abraham, "Why did Sarah laugh and say, 'Will I really have a child, now that I am old?' Is anything too hard for the Lord? I will return to you at the appointed time next year, and Sarah will have a son." Genesis 18:13-14

"No way!" Those two words have most likely escaped your mouth at some point in your life at the suggestion of something absurd, unlikely, or downright impossible. God made promises to Abraham that were hard to believe—too hard for Abraham's wife. But Abraham trusted in God's power to do the impossible. Because of his decision to live confidently in the promises of God, Abraham is known as the "Pioneer of Great Faith."

In the face of doubt, God states, "Is anything too hard for me?" Put that way, the answer is laughably obvious. To assume God can't do anything that he wants is to deny the very nature of his Godhood. As a man that follows God, you must in faith believe that God is capable, and trust in the character of his name. And when you face what appears to be an impossible circumstance, you must in faith believe that he can and will do great works.

God, I have some current situations in my life that are impossible for me to overcome—no way. But your power is unlimited. Strengthen my faith today in you and help me grow in my faith.

B
BEGIN: Why is this text so important?

U
UNPACK: What issues do you need to address?

I
INFORM: What does the text say to do?

L
LAND: What steps do you need to take?

D
DO: What action will you take today?

DISCOVER JOY

"Then he calls his friends and neighbors together and says, 'Rejoice with me; I have found my lost sheep.'" Luke 15:6

Jesus masterfully tells a parable about a shepherd who leaves a flock of ninety-nine sheep to find one that is lost. A shepherd has one duty: take care of sheep at all costs. The man went out to look for the stray because no loss was acceptable. This story stirs us to think about God's priorities.

Being like Jesus, or becoming his follower, means learning to have a heart like his and prioritizing the things he cares about. Because the Great Shepherd cares about those who are lost, spend some time praying for those who are wandering away from the flock. Align your heart with the great joy of knowing God's heart; be filled with compassion, not resentment, for those who are lost in this world.

God, as is common to selfish men, I focus mostly on my own needs. Today help me to have a heart more like yours, one for the lost of this world. Give me compassion and strength to love others as you have loved me.

BEGIN: Why is this text so important?

UNPACK: What issues do you need to address?

INFORM: What does the text say to do?

LAND: What steps do you need to take?

DO: What action will you take today?

EXAMINE SELF

Let us examine our ways and test them, and let us return to the Lord.
Lamentation 3:40

While we tend to just run at our days, it is often best to take a few minutes first to reflect and evaluate. The following are ten great questions to ask yourself if you wish to improve your spiritual life.

1. Are you spending daily time in the Scriptures and prayer?

2. Are you retaining impure thoughts that would not glorify God?

3. Are you honest in your financial dealings?

4. Are you investing time with family and friends?

5. Are you giving your 100% best in all environments?

6. Are you honest with those around you?

7. Are you sharing the good news with others?

8. Are you taking care of yourself physically?

9. Are you allowing people or circumstances to rob you of joy?

10. Have you just been completely honest in your answers?

God, as I reflect on these questions I invite you to examine me and the ways of my heart. If there are places I have gone wayward, bring me back to you.

B
BEGIN: Why is this text so important?

U
UNPACK: What issues do you need to address?

I
INFORM: What does the text say to do?

L
LAND: What steps do you need to take?

D
DO: What action will you take today?

ACKNOWLEDGE ABUNDANCE

"Now, our God, we give you thanks, and praise your glorious name. But who am I, and who are my people, that we should be able to give as generously as this? Everything comes from you, and we have given you only what comes from your hand." 1 Chronicles 29:13-14

In the moment above, David is transitioning the nation from his rule to that of his son Solomon. God had designated Solomon as the king who would build the temple, God's dwelling place among his people. Solomon is set to be a great leader like his father. Israel's wealth is overflowing. This is to be the high point in Israel's history, the very pinnacle of their success, and David responds with great humility as he speaks to God. His example is one worth emulating.

These words give you an idea of how you ought to respond to God when blessed with abundance. Times of abundance will come and go, and David realized that it all came from God and not from his efforts, wisdom, skill, or strength. God extended extravagant generosity, and David had nothing of his own to give, for he knew one crucial principle: God owns it all. We are only stewards during our time on earth. You can hear a subtle voice of great humility coming from a man adorned and blessed with excessive wealth.

God, I praise you for every abundance in my life. You are the first giver, and I am only a steward. I pray that you will help me give sacrificially from the abundances of my life, and live daily in gratefulness and humility for the opportunities and riches you have given me.

B

BEGIN: Why is this text so important?

U

UNPACK: What issues do you need to address?

I

INFORM: What does the text say to do?

L

LAND: What steps do you need to take?

D

DO: What action will you take today?

CONFIDENT BATTLE

Finally, be strong in the Lord and in the strength of his might. Put on the whole armor of God, that you may be able to stand against the schemes of the devil. For we do not wrestle against flesh and blood, but against the rulers, against the authorities, against the cosmic powers over this present darkness, against the spiritual forces of evil in the heavenly places. Therefore take up the whole armor of God, that you may be able to withstand in the evil day, and having done all, to stand firm. Ephesians 6:10-13

You are engaged in an ongoing spiritual battle. Whether you see it or not, it is happening around you. Paul urges you to be strong, to understand the nature of the struggle, and to take up the needed weaponry. This battle is not physical and therefore requires weapons from a spiritual arsenal. And God provides for you the tools needed to withstand the conflict.

In the end, the Bible tells us that the battle is won. It's a no-win for evil and a victory for those who stand with God. But there still is a battle that every man must fight. Jude 3:3 says it this way: "I found it necessary to write appealing to you to contend for the faith." Don't be passive today. Start arming yourself with the truth, and enter the battle against evil with the confidence that you have already won.

God, I do forget that the battle is won. Help me battle with confidence today on your behalf. Arm me with truth not against other men, but against evil, and I pray you will give me weapons of defense and offense when the moment is right.

B

BEGIN: Why is this text so important?

U

UNPACK: What issues do you need to address?

I

INFORM: What does the text say to do?

L

LAND: What steps do you need to take?

D

DO: What action will you take today?

VALUE SACRIFICE

"All this, O king, Araunah gives to the king." And Araunah said to the king, "May the Lord your God accept you." But the king said to Araunah, "No, but I will buy it from you for a price. I will not offer burnt offerings to the Lord my God that cost me nothing." So David bought the threshing floor and the oxen for fifty shekels of silver. 2 Samuel 24:23-24

The "house money effect" is a gambling phenomenon that occurs when a gambler recklessly bets away his previous winnings. Think of it like spending someone else's money. "House money" refers to chips or coins that belonged to the casino at the beginning of the night. If you get your hands on it, it's a lucky surplus, and easier to part with than the wages you earned. But in the above text, David refuses to play with the "house money."

Something offered free of cost rarely holds any true value. King David understood that sacrifices to the Lord in particular must have a cost or they would be meaningless. It was a matter of integrity. In this situation, David was presenting a sacrifice in response to his sin, and he would "pay" for it. Araunah was willing to give David the equivalent of "house money," but David declined, recognizing that he would have devalued both Araunah's gift and David's sacrifice for his sin. To make a valid and valuable sacrifice, it had to cost David something.

God, thanks for all the free gifts you give me. In light of this, today I am choosing to make small sacrifices on your behalf. Receive them as an offering to you in gratitude for the value you have added to my life.

B
_____

BEGIN: Why is this text so important?

U
_____

UNPACK: What issues do you need to address?

I
_____

INFORM: What does the text say to do?

L
_____

LAND: What steps do you need to take?

D
_____

DO: What action will you take today?

GET FEEDBACK

The ear that listens to life-giving reproof will dwell among the wise. Whoever ignores instruction despises himself, but he who listens to reproof gains intelligence. Proverbs 15:31-32

Reproof can be painful. It is important to consider that what is painful is not always harmful. It can have benefits. It is painful to have a tooth cavity filled, but in the end, it relieves pain and prevents further damage. In the same way, reproof in accountability relationships can be uncomfortable yet helpful at the same time. Without it, men are vulnerable to significant pain and further injury. Men learn to embrace reproof by others because we cannot afford an accountability deficit.

"Reproof" is accountability, not just from anyone, but from godly and wise men that you invite to evaluate your life. The payoff for you is intelligence, and the cost is willingness. Men that diligently live under accountability will enjoy accelerated spiritual growth—"they dwell among the wise." Stop ignoring the instruction of wise people in your life and start inviting, listening to, and applying their feedback. A deficit of accountability is no different than self-hatred.

God, I prefer autonomy, not accountability. Give me the courage to lean into accountability by inviting godly and wise men to observe and speak into my life.

B

BEGIN: Why is this text so important?

U

UNPACK: What issues do you need to address?

I

INFORM: What does the text say to do?

L

LAND: What steps do you need to take?

D

DO: What action will you take today?

INTENTION

The one who does what is sinful is of the devil, because the devil has been sinning from the beginning. The reason the Son of God appeared was to destroy the devil's work. No one who is born of God will continue to sin, because God's seed remains in them; they cannot go on sinning, because they have been born of God. This is how we know who the children of God are and who the children of the devil are: Anyone who does not do what is right is not God's child, nor is anyone who does not love their brother and sister.

1 John 3:8-10

The moment you decided to follow Jesus, you made it your mission to let him transform and sanctify your desires and your pursuits. With best intentions, you pledged to act in whatever way God asked you to. And hopefully this is still your heart's motivation: to repent from sinful habits and desires and devote your energy to God's kingdom. But maintaining good intentions is only the starting point. Because a desire to do what is right is not the same as actually doing it. God wants you to move beyond good intentions and act on his Word in faith.

James, the brother of Jesus, says it this way: "If anyone, then, knows the good they ought to do and doesn't do it, it is a sin for them" (James 4:17). The most prominent challenge you face is moving from intention to action. While we are all sinners saved by the grace of God, not by any effort of our own, we are expected to act in righteousness because of what was done for us. Strive to move beyond good intention, and act with convictions.

God, I confess that I often embrace inaction. I feel convicted but I do not live with conviction. This needs to change. Today I commit to bridging this gap between intention and action.

BEGIN: Why is this text so important?

UNPACK: What issues do you need to address?

INFORM: What does the text say to do?

LAND: What steps do you need to take?

DO: What action will you take today?

DRAW A LINE

Now fear the Lord and serve him with all faithfulness. Throw away the gods your ancestors worshiped beyond the Euphrates River and in Egypt, and serve the Lord. But if serving the Lord seems undesirable to you, then choose for yourselves this day whom you will serve, whether the gods your ancestors served beyond the Euphrates, or the gods of the Amorites, in whose land you are living. But as for me and my household, we will serve the Lord.
Joshua 24:14-15

Joshua gathered all the leaders of all the people of Israel to give them one final charge in the land of promise. He had long been a leader who modeled the importance of spiritual leadership and taking spiritual responsibility. Here he speaks plainly about the options and draws a clear line in the sand. And he does not leave those around him guessing on which side of the line he stands.

A man who will abide anything in truth stands for nothing. Joshua was not such a man. He decisively picked a spiritual side and took personal responsibility for it. Consider what spiritual stance you need to take in your daily life and model it for those around you. Inspire others to decide by making your decision clear.

God, I will no longer waver between opinions. I will pick a side. Help me have the courage to stand and let me inspire others to do so as well.

B

BEGIN: Why is this text so important?

U

UNPACK: What issues do you need to address?

I

INFORM: What does the text say to do?

L

LAND: What steps do you need to take?

D

DO: What action will you take today?

KEEP IN STEP

If we live by the Spirit, let us also keep in step with the Spirit. Let us not become conceited, provoking one another, envying one another. Galatians 5:25-26

Do two walk together unless they have agreed to do so? Amos 3:3

"Keep up with me." Have you ever gone for a walk, hike, or bike ride with someone who couldn't seem to keep up? Lose someone enough times, and you'll start to lose patience. We're often on the other end of that equation with the Holy Spirit. God sent us his Spirit as our leader and guide, and he's trying to call to us and show us the way forward. But for this to work, we must remain in step with him.

Keeping in step with the Spirit means that as he moves, you move. Stay close, and you won't have to worry about wandering off into dangerous terrain or getting lost by heading down the wrong path. You started off on the right track when you began your Christian journey, but it isn't a path you can navigate alone. Pay careful attention to the way the Spirit leads today. It may be that he's been trying to get your attention and change your course.

God, my path is not always your path. Sometimes I find myself taking my eyes off you. Help me focus on you today. Keep my eyes locked! And God, bless the ways of my spiritual feet as I listen more carefully today to the Spirit's voice. Be my leader and guide me.

B_____
BEGIN: Why is this text so important?

U_____
UNPACK: What issues do you need to address?

I_____
INFORM: What does the text say to do?

L_____
LAND: What steps do you need to take?

D_____
DO: What action will you take today?

WISDOM LISTENING

The proverbs of Solomon son of David, king of Israel: for gaining wisdom and instruction; for understanding words of insight; for receiving instruction in prudent behavior, doing what is right and just and fair; for giving prudence to those who are simple, knowledge and discretion to the young—let the wise listen and add to their learning, and let the discerning get guidance.
Proverbs 1:1-5

Solomon was the wisest man ever to have lived. God invited him to ask for anything he wanted, and Solomon asked for an understanding and discerning heart. In a display of God's pleasure with such a request, he granted young Solomon wisdom and a lot more. And so when a man like Solomon writes about how to gain understanding, it's best to take heed.

Wisdom proceeds from listening, and there are all kinds of benefits. And even better, listening is a stackable activity—there is no limit on how much wisdom you can obtain by listening. The best practice for growing wise is not exercising your own knowledge, maturing your gifts, or even pursuing greater credibility—it's listening to others. Any man can become wise regardless of age, status, or season of life. And every area of your life can be impacted by this increase in wisdom. Take Solomon's word for it and receive this life-changing advice.

God, I may not be a great listener, but I'm willing to learn. I want to grow in wisdom, and I pray like Solomon prayed that you would make me a wise man. Let me be wiser today than yesterday through active listening—to you, and to the wisdom of others.

BEGIN: Why is this text so important?

UNPACK: What issues do you need to address?

INFORM: What does the text say to do?

LAND: What steps do you need to take?

DO: What action will you take today?

DEEP INTEGRITY

Now Joseph was well-built and handsome, and after a while his master's wife took notice of Joseph and said, "Come to bed with me!" But he refused. "With me in charge," he told her, "my master does not concern himself with anything in the house; everything he owns he has entrusted to my care. No one is greater in this house than I am. My master has withheld nothing from me except you, because you are his wife. How then could I do such a wicked thing and sin against God?" And though she spoke to Joseph day after day, he refused to go to bed with her or even be with her. Genesis 39:7-10

How does a man stand up under repeated attacks on his integrity? Joseph is an excellent example. He was a man who was far away from his home country, his people, and everything that would have represented accountability. In the midst of temptation, Joseph did not waver. In front of him was an enticing offer that did not cause him to stumble or falter.

The lesson to learn from this man of integrity is to ground your integrity deep. Joseph's integrity was tested daily, but he dug in deeper and deeper with each advance. His integrity was not founded on his master's supervision, teaching, or presence, but on God and on God's principles. Joseph's insatiable desire to obey God allowed him to resist and reject the woman's appeal to his sexual appetites. If your integrity were tested, where and when would it fail? The foundation of your integrity should be the power of God within you, not the absence of temptation around you. But build on that foundation with some personal accountability. Although Joseph endured alone, you are surrounded by fellow believers—take advantage of that blessing. Let your desire to honor God fuel your steadfast commitment to integrity.

God, today I am going to commit to maintaining my integrity. In everything I do, I pray my integrity will stand firm. And God, know my secret ways and guide me back when I am tempted to compromise.

B_____

BEGIN: Why is this text so important?

U_____

UNPACK: What issues do you need to address?

I_____

INFORM: What does the text say to do?

L_____

LAND: What steps do you need to take?

D_____

DO: What action will you take today?

DISCERNMENT

The Israelites sampled their provisions but did not inquire of the Lord. Then Joshua made a treaty of peace with them to let them live, and the leaders of the assembly ratified it by oath. Three days after they made the treaty with the Gibeonites, the Israelites heard that they were neighbors, living near them.
Joshua 9:14-16

Israel had wild success in the battles against Jericho and Ai. The mission was simple: divide and conquer. As neighboring cities got wind of what was going on, they were terrified. Instead of fighting an army backed by the Living God, their best hope was to stage a ruse—to trick Israel into signing a treaty. The trickery was simple: they dressed themselves in worn-out clothes and put moldy food in their packs. The Israelites took one look at the costumes and props, and were convinced that these people lived in a far-off land and posed no threat. So they entered into an agreement with the very enemy they had been instructed to destroy.

Have you ever agreed to something you later regretted? Have you acted on an offer that looked fair, but in the end was terrible? The lesson to learn from Joshua is this: inquire of the Lord and work with discernment. Joshua made a crucial leadership decision without talking to God. And that decision had all sorts of consequences. As you lead, in whatever context you may find yourself, learn from Joshua's example. Stop relying on your own assessment. Grow your discernment by inquiring of the Lord.

God, discernment is something I need, but I also need to bring my need for insight to you. Please help me to bring my dilemmas to you with courage and confidence, not taking pride in my own judgment or understanding but seeking your wisdom and perspective.

B

BEGIN: Why is this text so important?

U

UNPACK: What issues do you need to address?

I

INFORM: What does the text say to do?

L

LAND: What steps do you need to take?

D

DO: What action will you take today?

FREE MAN

Likewise, my brothers, you also have died to the law through the body of Christ, so that you may belong to another, to him who has been raised from the dead, in order that we may bear fruit for God. For while we were living in the flesh, our sinful passions, aroused by the law, were at work in our members to bear fruit for death. But now we are released from the law, having died to that which held us captive, so that we serve in the new way of the Spirit and not in the old way of the written code. Romans 7:4-6

When a man dies, he is released from the responsibilities of this life. There is no longer any obligation to pay taxes, maintain a property, or serve an earthly authority. Nothing at all is required of a dead man. Paul explains to us here how Christ's death becomes our death. Through the death of Christ, the fulfillment of our obligation to the law is complete.

Jesus' death and resurrection are applied to those who receive him and believe in his name. You are free from the law and now open to the new way of God's Spirit. You are no longer held captive to what the law requires. Your new life is one that follows the Spirit of the Living God. And here is what you are freed to do: to "keep in step" with him. An enormous burden has been lifted, and you can dedicate every action to Christ instead of acting in service to worldly concerns. Enjoy your spiritual freedom.

God, I often don't realize the benefits of my freedom. I need and want this freedom, but I usually only see the bondage of the law of sin that works in me. Help me to enjoy the freedom of your Spirit today. May I live in victory over spiritual and physical death.

B
_____

BEGIN: Why is this text so important?

U
_____

UNPACK: What issues do you need to address?

I
_____

INFORM: What does the text say to do?

L
_____

LAND: What steps do you need to take?

D
_____

DO: What action will you take today?

TRUTH SPOKEN

When the governor motioned for him to speak, Paul replied: "I know that for a number of years you have been a judge over this nation; so I gladly make my defense. You can easily verify that no more than twelve days ago I went up to Jerusalem to worship. My accusers did not find me arguing with anyone at the temple, or stirring up a crowd in the synagogues or anywhere else in the city. And they cannot prove to you the charges they are now making against me. However, I admit that I worship the God of our ancestors as a follower of the Way, which they call a sect. I believe everything that is in accordance with the Law and that is written in the Prophets, and I have the same hope in God as these men themselves have, that there will be a resurrection of both the righteous and the wicked. So I strive always to keep my conscience clear before God and man." Acts 24:10-16

The defendant always spoke after the accuser in Roman trials, and this holds true in the passage above.   Tertullus presented numerous untrue facts to the governor, none of which phased Paul. When Paul was permitted to speak, he began by appealing to the governor's sense of justice. Truthfully and with precision, Paul laid out his defense. He knew and leveraged a leadership tool that every man should use.

Paul used integrity and truth in the face of deceit and inaccuracy. Great men know how to plainly speak the truth without being baited into anger. Learning this art and speaking the truth in all circumstances will build you as a man. Find ways to engage in this this behavior frequently, no matter the situation.

God, like Paul, I know what it is like to be harassed, persecuted, or falsely accused. Help my integrity to mitigate my need for justice, and I pray today that I will have peace in my next moment of trial.

BEGIN: Why is this text so important?

UNPACK: What issues do you need to address?

INFORM: What does the text say to do?

LAND: What steps do you need to take?

DO: What action will you take today?

KNOW YOUR PRIDE

Pride goes before destruction and a haughty spirit before a fall. Proverbs 16:18

Men who accomplish an extraordinary level of prosperity, prestige, or position can become immortalized by the world. Consider for a moment one well-known athlete, business leader, author, or speaker. Sometimes these men of elevated stature develop a distorted view of self and the world around them. Surely you can think of more than one example of a man whose fame has gone to his head.

But a man who knows his pride, and knows when and how it manifests itself, can humble himself before the pride distorts his view of self and damages his identity, character, and relationships. One of Jesus' outstanding qualities was his ability to acknowledge his status and position of great power while persistently redirecting attention away from himself to his Father. You should follow this example and do the same before you fall flat on your face.

God, help me to live humbly and keep my pose, posture, and position subject to you. I know pride can be elusive, so help me to become aware of its tactics. I submit all I am to you.

B_____

BEGIN: Why is this text so important?

U_____

UNPACK: What issues do you need to address?

I_____

INFORM: What does the text say to do?

L_____

LAND: What steps do you need to take?

D_____

DO: What action will you take today?

BE OBEDIENT

The Lord had said to Abram, "Go from your country, your people and your father's household to the land I will show you. I will make you into a great nation, and I will bless you; I will make your name great, and you will be a blessing. I will bless those who bless you, and whoever curses you I will curse; and all peoples on earth will be blessed through you." So Abram went, as the Lord had told him; and Lot went with him. Abram was seventy-five years old when he set out from Harran. He took his wife Sarai, his nephew Lot, all the possessions they had accumulated and the people they had acquired in Harran, and they set out for the land of Canaan, and they arrived there.
Genesis 12:1-5

Abram's life is an exceptional story of God calling a man on an incredible journey. The description of how God called Abram gives us insight into how God calls us today. The words "great" and "bless," repeated numerous times, reveal the heart of the God to Abram. What's missing are all the details between Abram's faithful departure and God's eventual blessing. Abram did not let the unknown keep him from obediently following God.

You can expect God to call you to great things. Abram's calling may be different from yours, but God's heart and character have not changed. He may not lay out every detail of the road ahead, but he will bless faithful obedience. The Bible doesn't describe any hesitation from Abram; he went all-in from the first moment. As you discern the direction in which God is leading you, do not get hung up on the details. Be wise and demonstrate courage when you step out. Obedience along the way is the measure of success, not knowledge of all the details.

God, I may not know the future, but as Abram illustrates, I can take one step of obedience today. Help me to be obedient today and then tomorrow and the day after.

B

———————————————

BEGIN: Why is this text so important?

U

———————————————

UNPACK: What issues do you need to address?

I

———————————————

INFORM: What does the text say to do?

L

———————————————

LAND: What steps do you need to take?

D

———————————————

DO: What action will you take today?

FAILURE TEACHES

Have mercy on me, O God, according to your steadfast love; according to your abundant mercy blot out my transgressions. Wash me thoroughly from my iniquity, and cleanse me from my sin! For I know my transgressions, and my sin is ever before me. Against you, you only, have I sinned and done what is evil in your sight, so that you may be justified in your words and blameless in your judgment. Behold, I was brought forth in iniquity, and in sin did my mother conceive me. Behold, you delight in truth in the inward being, and you teach me wisdom in the secret heart. Psalm 51:1-6

Psalm 51 is a powerful prayer from a man wrecked by sin. King David had done the unthinkable and left a blood trail in his life and the lives of those around him. Aware of his need for forgiveness and course correction, he demonstrates why he's known for being a man after God's heart. David models an openness to God that allows truth to reveal his wrongdoing and simultaneously teach him wisdom. Failure and pain become great teachers when a man is vulnerable before God.

Benjamin Franklin said it this way: "Those things that hurt, instruct." A man who allows the pain of sin to drive him toward real repentance learns profound wisdom. Therefore, becoming wise requires that you reflect in and through the pain the same way that David did. Acknowledging and taking inventory of your actions before God will make you into a better man. Do not be afraid to address your failures. Instead of letting shame stunt your spiritual growth, use your failures as a tool to shape your character.

God, today I think about my failures. Help me to overcome my shame. Give me the strength to reflect on what happened, confess my weakness, repent from my poor choices, and never repeat them. May I learn the lessons you are teaching me, and may I live victoriously in a new day.

BEGIN: Why is this text so important?

UNPACK: What issues do you need to address?

INFORM: What does the text say to do?

LAND: What steps do you need to take?

DO: What action will you take today?

OBEY COURAGEOUSLY

Eli's sons were scoundrels; they had no regard for the Lord. 1 Samuel 2:12

And the Lord said to Samuel: "See, I am about to do something in Israel that will make the ears of everyone who hears about it tingle. At that time I will carry out against Eli everything I spoke against his family—from beginning to end. For I told him that I would judge his family forever because of the sin he knew about; his sons blasphemed God, and he failed to restrain them. Therefore I swore to the house of Eli, 'The guilt of Eli's house will never be atoned for by sacrifice or offering.'" 1 Samuel 3:11-14

During the days of Eli, God rarely spoke directly to his people. Even though there were very few fresh visions from God, Moses had written down what God had shown him, and so the priest Eli knew how to carry out his God-given tasks faithfully. Despite knowing what to do, Eli's sons blatantly disregarded God. The real tragedy of this story is that Eli didn't intervene. As their father and the spiritual leader of God's people, God held Eli accountable for his lack of response to an ugly situation.

It is common to judge people based on their actions. But this story illustrates that failure to act can also have a significant consequence. James says it this way: "Remember, it is a sin to know what you ought to do and then not do it" (James 4:17). Had Eli mustered the courage to do what he knew was right, the outcome would have been much different. So replace cowardice with courage, and ready yourself for action. In the face of challenge, get in the game. Remind yourself that God looks for men committed to faithful obedience.

God, I will have opportunities today to be courageous. Help me to act, especially when I see injustice and sin, and may I respond in a way that honors and represents you. Help me to fight the impulse to be apathetic.

B
———————————————
BEGIN: Why is this text so important?

U
———————————————
UNPACK: What issues do you need to address?

I
———————————————
INFORM: What does the text say to do?

L
———————————————
LAND: What steps do you need to take?

D
———————————————
DO: What action will you take today?

FOCUSED TASK

So we built the wall. And all the wall was joined together to half its height, for the people had a mind to work. But when Sanballat and Tobiah and the Arabs and the Ammonites and the Ashdodites heard that the repairing of the walls of Jerusalem was going forward and that the breaches were beginning to be closed, they were outraged. And they all plotted together to come and fight against Jerusalem and to cause confusion in it. And we prayed to our God and set a guard as a protection against them day and night. Nehemiah 4:6-8

Nehemiah set out to complete a task. He began to rebuild Jerusalem's wall, closing the breaches. The people working with him had a determined mindset that allowed for progress, but very few endeavors like this go without distraction. Halfway through the project, Nehemiah and the builders had to face off against a group of angry individuals conspiring to undermine their work. His response to this distraction should be noted and copied by all men.

Nehemiah's first response to this threat was prayer. By recognizing God's power and authority, Nehemiah demonstrated his dependence on God. If the work was to be successful, it would be through God's strength and mercy, not human determination. The next move Nehemiah made was preventative. The work was important and worth protecting, so he guarded it. He did not overreact or let this distraction uproot him from the task at hand. You must guard against diversion while working on your God-given responsibilities. Don't let distractions confuse you; become a man like Nehemiah who depends on God, takes appropriate action, and moves forward.

God, I am often distracted by the things of this world, including career opportunities and crises, idle pleasures, money concerns, and the like. Help me be undistracted today, focusing on you and your pleasures, not my own—so that your efforts will be built up.

B _____

BEGIN: Why is this text so important?

U _____

UNPACK: What issues do you need to address?

I _____

INFORM: What does the text say to do?

L _____

LAND: What steps do you need to take?

D _____

DO: What action will you take today?

SPEAK BOLDLY

His disciples said, "Ah, now you are speaking plainly and not using figurative speech! Now we know that you know all things and do not need anyone to question you; this is why we believe that you came from God." Jesus answered them, "Do you now believe? Behold, the hour is coming, indeed it has come, when you will be scattered, each to his own home, and will leave me alone. Yet I am not alone, for the Father is with me. I have said these things to you, that in me you may have peace. In the world you will have tribulation. But take heart; I have overcome the world." John 16:29-33

Think for a moment about why Jesus spoke these words to his disciples. As a leader of men, Jesus understood the big picture and knew what his men needed to hear. The disciples were about to face challenging times. We have the luxury of knowing how Jesus was about to conquer sin and death, but at this moment in time, these men did not foresee what was ahead of them. Great leaders are aware of rising tension, but leverage the big picture to encourage those around them.

Billy Graham once said, "I have read the last page of the Bible. It's all going to turn out all right." It's important, even crucial, to attend to troubling circumstances as a leader. Jesus noted this with his men and didn't sugar-coat reality. The next thing he did is a best practice all men should emulate: Jesus knew and boldly stated why his disciples should have courage. When trials creep into your life, attend to them but do not focus on them. Start reminding yourself and those around you of the victory to come.

God, I want to lead others in your name. Today I am going to charge into my day confident of the outcome, armed with boldness. But boldness not for my own pursuits, boldness for you.

B
_____

BEGIN: Why is this text so important?

U
_____

UNPACK: What issues do you need to address?

I
_____

INFORM: What does the text say to do?

L
_____

LAND: What steps do you need to take?

D
_____

DO: What action will you take today?

LOOK RIGHT

Joab saw that there were battle lines in front of him and behind him; so he selected some of the best troops in Israel and deployed them against the Arameans. He put the rest of the men under the command of Abishai his brother and deployed them against the Ammonites. Joab said, "If the Arameans are too strong for me, then you are to come to my rescue; but if the Ammonites are too strong for you, then I will come to rescue you. Be strong, and let us fight bravely for our people and the cities of our God. The Lord will do what is good in his sight." 2 Samuel 10:9-12

In the heat of battle, it is crucial that a leader looks in two different directions. Joab first looked forward at the gathering threat and the fighting men that he was responsible to deploy. Based on what he saw, he selected the best men for the job. Then Joab looked to the rear and saw another force to repel. Upon his observation, he gave a clear call to action, inspiring his men to see the big picture—they were about to defend their people and the cities of God.

It is easy to get caught looking in the wrong direction. Only look ahead, and you will miss opportunities to inspire those around you. If you focus solely on those you lead, you will fail to chart a clear course. And don't forget there are plenty of distractions that can wholly undermine your effectiveness as a leader. The key is to be balanced, which requires a disciplined mind and resolute determination. Be like Joab and look in the most critical directions whether working alone or leading others.

God, do what is right in your eyes today. May I be prepared for the battle on all sides. Direct my focus and my actions.

B
BEGIN: Why is this text so important?

U
UNPACK: What issues do you need to address?

I
INFORM: What does the text say to do?

L
LAND: What steps do you need to take?

D
DO: What action will you take today?